T0072028

READING WITH ANIMAL MINI-BOOKS

READING WITH ANIMAL MINI-BOOKS

Learn to Read and Write with Rhyming Word Families

Celeste Meiergerd

Text copyright © 2021 Celeste Meiergerd. Design and concept copyright © 2021 Ulysses Press and its licensors. All rights reserved. Any unauthorized duplication in whole or in part or dissemination of this edition by any means (including but not limited to photocopying, electronic devices, digital versions, and the internet) will be prosecuted to the fullest extent of the law.

Published in the United States by:
Ulysses Press
PO Box 3440
Berkeley, CA 94703
www.ulyssespress.com

ISBN: 978-1-64604-253-1
Library of Congress Control Number: 2021937753

Printed in the United States by Kingery Printing Company
10 9 8 7 6 5 4 3 2 1

Acquisitions editor: Casie Vogel
Managing editor: Claire Chun
Editor: Pat Harris
Proofreader: Joyce Wu
Front cover design: Jake Flaherty
Interior design: what!design @ whatweb.com and Jake Flaherty
Production: Jake Flaherty
Cover art: tiger © GraphicsRF.com/shutterstock.com; giraffe © White Space Illustrations/shutterstock.com
Interior art: shutterstock.com

CONTENTS

Introduction 1

The Books

The Dad (-ad word family) 7

Rabbit Digs (-ag word family) 9

Sam the Ram (-am word family) 11

Dolphin and Dan (-an word family) 13

Monkey and the Map (-ap word family) 15

Cat and Rat (-at word family) 17

That Fat Bat (-at word family) 19

Fox (-ed word family) 21

Jen and the Ten Hens (-en word family) 23

Betty's Pet Bird (-et word family) 25

Pig in a Wig (-ig word family) 27

Shark Race (-in word family) 29

Alligator Swim (-ip word family) 31

Hippo (-it word family) 33

Kangaroo Hops (-op word family) 35

Giraffe's Spots (-ot word family) 37

Clean Cub (-ub word family) 39

The Bug (-ug word family) 41

A Squirrel (-ut word family) 43
Snail Mail (-ail word family) 45
Baking Snake (-ake word family) 47
The Wolf's Fang (-ang word family) 49
Mark at the Park (-ark word family) 51
The Deer (-ate word family) 53
The Turtle (-ell word family). 55
The Three Mice (-ice word family) 57
The Cheetah (-ick word family) 59
What Do You See? (-ill word family) 61
King Penguin (-ing word family) 63
A Fish's Wish (-ish word family) 65
The Zebra (-ock word family) 67
Flamingo Music (-ong word family) 69
The Owl (-ight word family) 71

Acknowledgments 73

About the Author 74

INTRODUCTION

What to Expect in This Workbook

Encourage early reading and writing skills as well as recognition of different word families among your young learners with the *Reading with Animal Mini-Books* workbook! *Reading with Animal Mini-Books* is a workbook full of removable mini-books ready to be carefully crafted by children and students ranging from preschool to first grade. All of the mini-books center on the practice of essential early literacy skills through reading and writing familiar sight words in basic word families. The stories emphasize the use of simple CVC (consonant, vowel, consonant) words, such as "cat" and "map," to make them applicable for the earliest readers. As the workbook advances from mini-book to mini-book, the complexity of the word families and the words used in the stories increase in difficulty as well. This slow buildup allows for the greatest chance of success among the intended ages, as well as ease for an adult to find the perfect mini-book at the desired level.

The Importance of Learning through Word Families

Children learn through exposure and repetition. This is why they can "read" familiar brands while walking through the grocery store or understand an advertisement in a magazine before they even know their letter sounds. When the use of word families is incorporated into early reading practice, children are more likely to recognize and recall what particular word endings look and sound like.

When reading, if children are able to recall an ending sound, it is much easier for them to sound out a potential new word, as they have to sound out only the beginning part of the word. As they see the similar word endings within the stories in these mini-books, they will begin to make connections to how the words are read.

What Makes This Workbook Special

This workbook is perfect for early readers because of its repetitive nature. The mini-books are similar in the way they progress, with each page building on the previous one. This allows the young readers to really understand what each word is before seeing a new word appear. Unlike flash cards, which can be dull for a young child, this workbook provides repetition in a fun and engaging way.

Each page includes young children's favorite animals and memorable rhymes that make reading fun and interesting. The rhyming scheme on each page makes the reading feel lyrical—allowing for children to begin recognizing which sounds different letter combinations make in each word. With over thirty unique mini-books ready to be made, and each page featuring young children's favorite animals acting out silly scenes, the learning of each word family is distinct and unforgettable. The black-and-white pages invite young children to color, write, and read their very own mini-book creations, allowing them to be in control of their own learning with the ability to create.

Additionally, the activities woven into the mini-books provide enough instruction for children to maintain accuracy in the content they're learning and achieving. Traceable letters with exact sizing and fill-in-the-blank letters for words previously seen in a story allow for higher chances of success for every child at every reading level. Children are gifted with the opportunity to feel that they are writing their own stories and to feel success when they see it all come together with that special touch of their favorite colors and their own handwriting. Once the mini-book is filled in and ready to read, the pictures on the pages will provide context clues that allow young readers to strive toward successful, independent reading.

How to Use This Workbook

The format of this workbook leaves lots of room for flexibility in the way it is presented. The mini-books can be made by the specifications listed here: perfectly torn out, bound together, and ready to be filled in by a child with guidance, making use of favorite crayons, pencils, and markers. Or, for more advanced learners, children can be encouraged to independently write, tear, and put together their own books.

These mini-books focus on numerous basic word families and are applicable for working with an individual child or can be copied for multiple students' use. Although this workbook emphasizes children's independence and self-confidence in their reading and writing skills, having an adult as part of their experience can make a dramatic impact on how successful they are. This workbook is a great fit for both the prepared parent and the knowledgeable teacher, both striving to enrich a

child's learning to prepare for those first days of school and to spark creativity in the way students transition to independent readers.

Time to get started. Let's make some books!

How to Put the Mini-Books Together

The pages in the *Reading with Animal Mini-Books* workbook include perforated edges for easy removal without any content being left behind through rips or tears. Putting each mini-book together is so simple with the help of the built-in perforated edges. These perforations are along each page of the mini-books and also along the overall binding of the entire workbook. The ease of these perforations allows for quick setup and removes the need for scissors! Here are the steps for making perfect mini-books every time:

- Simply tear out the sheet containing the book you want. Be sure to rip at the perforated edge located in the center of the book.

If you want to have multiple copies of a mini-book (for classroom use or otherwise), make a double-sided copy before going on to the next step.

Front **Back**

- Next, look for the perforated edge that separates the pages of the mini-book (if you are looking at the cover page, the perforated edge will split pages 5 and 8 as well as page 4 and the cover page). Rip along this perforated edge so that you have two separate sheets of paper.

Tear in half at the perforation

- Lay the pages on top of each other so that page 4 and 5 is on top of page 2 and 7.

- Line up these two papers so that they are even, and then fold in half along the middle seam of the pages so that the cover ends up facing you.

- Now you can bind the pages together. There are many ways to do this, but here are a few ideas:

  * Staple the pages together.

  * Hole punch the corner of the pages and have the child choose a special color of ribbon or yarn to tie the pages together.

  * Put brass tacks on the side for more movement of the pages.

  * The possibilities for binding are endless! Include children in the process to have them even more excited about creating their mini-books.

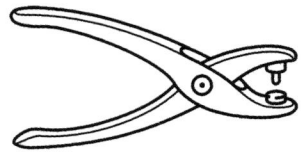

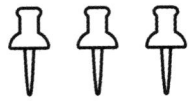

- And finally...it's done! The mini-book is ready to use.

The lad looks for Dad.

Is Dad mad?

Is Dad sad?

No, Dad is glad!

Where is Dad?

Here is the lad.

Rabbit Digs

ag

Rabbit finds a tag.

-ag Word Practice
ag
ag
ag
t w r

Rabbit puts
it in the bag.

Rabbit puts
it in the bag.

Rabbit's tail
starts to wag.

Rabbit finds a rag.

-am Word Practice

am

am

am

h j r

Sam likes ham.

Sam likes jam.

Sam is a ram.

Sam eats jam on ham.

Here is Sam.

Dolphin and Dan drive in a van.

Dolphin and Dan get a tan.

-an Word Practice

an

an

an

m v f

Dolphin is friends with Dan.

Dan is a man.

Dolphin and Dan need a fan.

Dolphin and Dan ran.

The map is in Monkey's lap.

Monkey sees a gap.

Monkey finds a map.

Monkey takes a nap.

Monkey wears a cap.

This is Rat.

Cat and Rat sat.

-at Word Practice

_____ at

_____ at

_____ at

r c m

This is Cat.

Cat and Rat sat
on a mat.

-at Word Practice

_____ at

_____ at

_____ at

f h b

That Fat Bat

I see a fat bat.

I see a hat.

at

That fat bat
wears a hat.

I see a bat.

Fox finds a sled!

-ed Word Practice

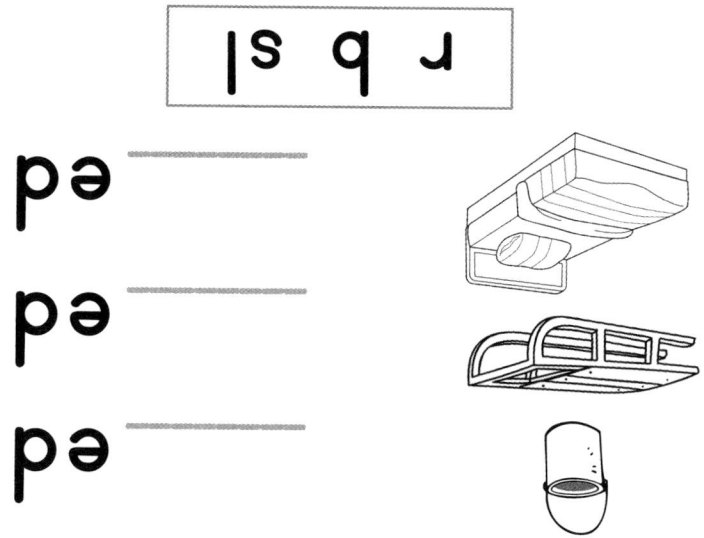

Fox paints the sled red.

Fox looks in the shed.

Fox sleeps in the bed.

Fox rides the red sled.

Jen and the Ten Hens

-en Word Practice

_____ en

_____ en

_____ en

p d h

Inside there is a hen.

Jen sees another hen. Jen counts the hens with a pen.

Jen opens the den.

Ten hens inside the den.

Betty's
Pet Bird

Betty gets
Bird wet.

-et Word Practice
et
et
et
w j n

Betty gets Bird a net.

What does
Betty get?

Betty gets Bird a jet.

Betty gets a pet!

Bird and Betty met.

-ig Word Practice

ig

ig

ig

p d j

The big pig
finds a wig.

The big pig will dig.

The pig is big.

The pig in a wig
does a jig.

Shark Race

They race to the bin.

-in Word Practice

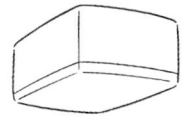

_____ in

_____ in

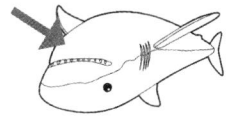

_____ in

f b ch

One shark bumps its chin.

in

I see one shark fin.

Who will win?

I see two.
It is a twin!

Alligator goes
for a dip.

Alligator puts in the tail's tip.

-ip Word Practice

_____ip

_____ip

_____ip

r s l

It is too cold. Alligator's body goes flip.

The water is on Alligator's lip.

Alligator hears the shorts go rip!

Alligator takes a sip.

sit

-it Word Practice

Will Hippo fit?

Hippo bit.

Hippo sits in a pit.

Hippo finds a kit.

-op Word Practice

op

op

op

t m p

Kangaroo Hops

Kangaroo hops on a top.

Kangaroo hops on a mop.

Watch Kangaroo hop.

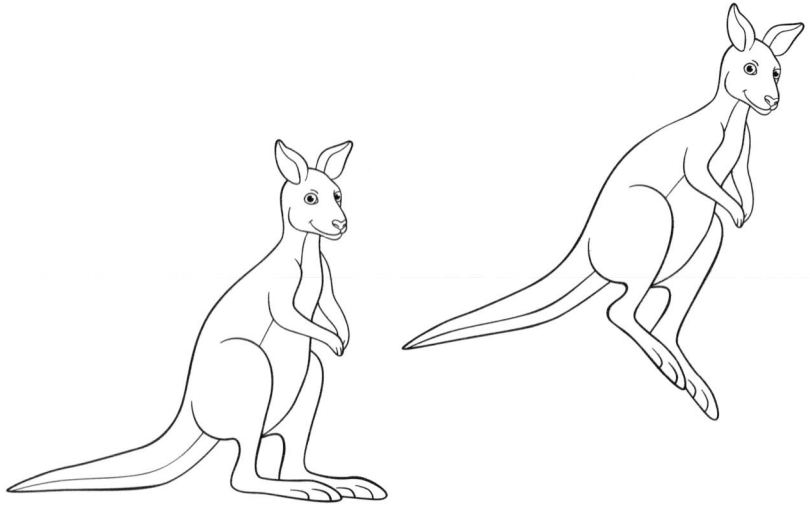

Kangaroo hears a pop.

Zebra tells Kangaroo, "Stop!"

Giraffe sees a spot.

On the spot is a dot.

-ot Word Practice

ot

ot

ot

c h p

Giraffe sleeps
on a cot.

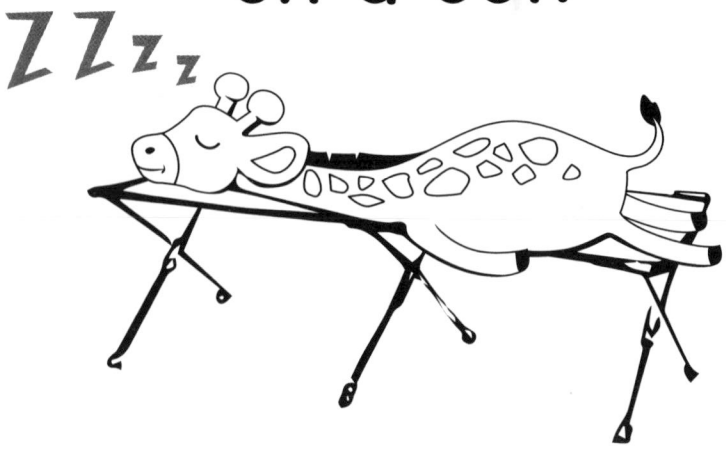

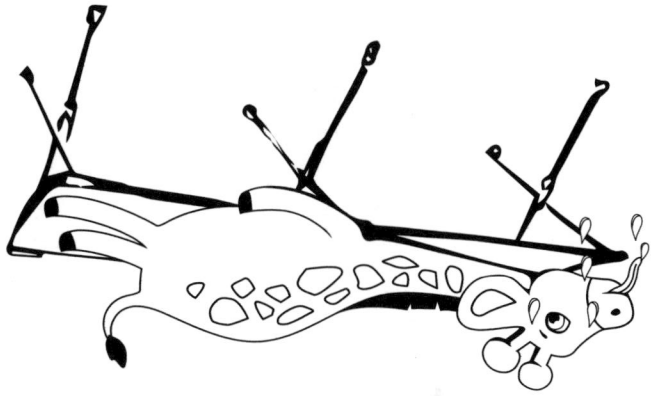

The cot got hot.

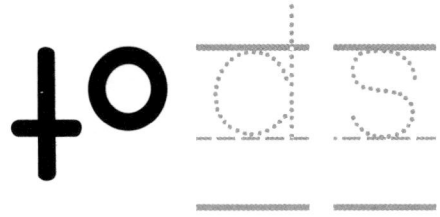

Giraffe counts the
spots. There are a lot!

-ub Word Practice

_____ ub

_____ ub

_____ ub

r t c

Clean Cub

ub

_____ _____ _____

Scrub, scrub, scrub.

Rub, rub, rub.

The cub climbs in the tub.

The cub is ready for the nature club.

I see the cub.

The Bug

The bug drinks
from a mug.

-ug Word Practice

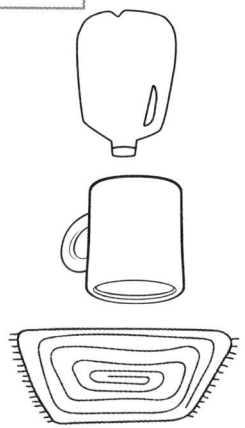

_____ ug

_____ ug

_____ ug

m r j

The bug lies on a rug.

The bug goes tug.

The bug pulls
out the jug.

The bug asks
for a hug.

The bug is snug
on the rug.

-ut Word Practice

_____ ut

_____ ut

n h

A squirrel feels a grumble in its gut.

A Squirrel

ut

A squirrel pushes the door until it is shut.

Time to go look for a nut!

A squirrel lives in a hut.

Snail Mail

Snail rides on a sail.

ail

-ail Word Practice
ail
ail
ail
p h m

Snail walks through hail.

Snail delivered the mail!

Snail walks by a tail.

Snail puts mail in the pail.

Baking
Snake

Will Snake bake
a rake?

No, Snake will
bake a cake!
350F

-ake Word Practice
ake
ake
ake
r c l

Snake takes the cake to the lake.

Snake eats cake with Jake.

350F°
?
What will Snake make?

350F°
Snake will bake.

The wolf pulls the
fang with a bang!

-ang Word Practice

ang

ang

f s

"No more fang,
the wolf sang!

Look at the
wolf's fang.

Look at that
fang hang.

Mark at
the Park

Mark sees a lark.

ark

-ark Word Practice
ark
ark
p d

Mark goes to the park.

I see a dog named Mark.

The park gets dark.

The deer ate.

The deer ate at
a fast rate.

-ate Word Practice

ate

ate

d g

ate

ate

The deer opened
the gate.

Oh, no! The deer
was late.

Outside the gate
was a date.

It hit the turtle's shell.

It made the turtle yell!

The turtle walked
to a well.

Inside the well was a bell!

-ice Word Practice

The nice mice
eat some rice.

Look at the mice.

They play with dice.

1 2 3

There are three mice.

Will the cheetah play with Nick or Rick?

Whom will the cheetah pick?

The cheetah feels sick.

The cheetah gives
Nick a lick.

The cheetah will
feel better quick.

What Do
You See?

Together, they all
walk up the hill.

Hedgehog says,
"Look at my quill!"

Fish says, "Look
at my gill!"

-ing Word Practice

k r d

_____ ing

_____ ing

_____ ing

He rings his bell with a ding.

The big ring is on the king's wing.

Penguin is a king.

The king wears a big ring.

King Penguin wants someone to sing.

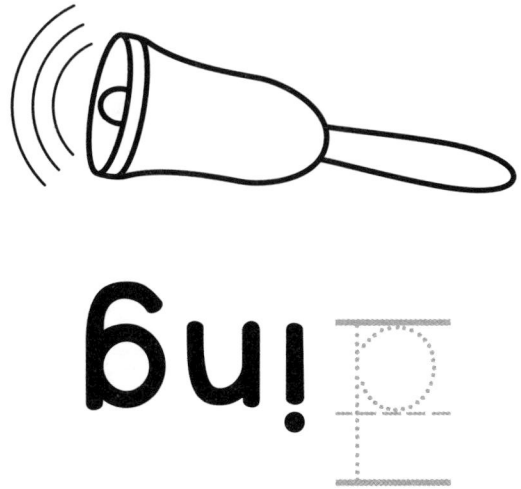

ing

The fish makes a wish.

In the bowl is a fish.

The fish wishes
for a dish.

Zebra asks for his sock.

Zebra trips on a rock.

Knock, knock, knock, knock.

Zebra makes it to the dock.

Zebra sees the lock.

Flamingo
Music

This flamingo
hits a gong.

gong

-ong Word Practice
ong
ong
ong
l s g

ong

The flamingo's
legs are so long.

This flamingo
sings a song.

ong

-ight Word Practice
ight
ight
ight
s r l

Owl flies to the right.

The Owl

ight

What a sight!

Owl flies at night.

Owl flies until
it is light.

Owl flies at a
great height.

ACKNOWLEDGMENTS

To my love and partner in life: thank you for all of your continued support throughout this entire process. Your ability to always have emotional space and time in your day to look at my progress and celebrate my victories has given me renewed confidence throughout this experience. I appreciate your support making my childhood dreams of being an author an actual reality.

To my family: all of those late nights in school of having you edit my papers and tweak my words to have them be my best is something that I wouldn't change for the world. Your constructive criticism has allowed me to get to this stage of publishing my second workbook, and I couldn't be more grateful for the time that has been invested from each and every one of you. Thank you for always pushing me to do the thing that is a challenge and for never allowing me to settle for the "easy way." This success was only possible because of you.

To past teachers and educators: I want to thank those teachers in my life who showcased my writing, took the time to look at my creations, or told me I could accomplish anything I set my mind to. I am forever grateful for your passion and the way that it has influenced my adult life and career.

ABOUT THE AUTHOR

Celeste Meiergerd is a self-contained special education preschool teacher located in Phoenix, Arizona. After graduating from Arizona State University in 2015 with her bachelor of arts in early childhood education and certification in special education, she began her teaching career. She has worked with a wide range of students, from two to five years of age, all displaying needs in the areas of communication, cognition, social-emotional regulation, adaptive skills, and motor abilities.

Student success is the driving force behind each thing she commits to in her career, as she hopes to inspire young minds in each of her endeavors. This is her second workbook, which follows *The Cars, Trucks, Trains, and Planes Pre-K Workbook*.